Educating and strengthening fearful and traumatized dogs

- Dog training practice book -

How to recognize fear and stress in your dog, interpret it correctly and treat it sensitively

Inga Dahlmann

CONTENTS

What you can expect in this book

Many dogs, especially those from animal shelters, have not had good experiences in their previous lives and are traumatized or fearful. This often manifests itself in different behaviors in different situations. For example, a dog expresses its fear through aggression on the lead if another dog comes too close, if it encounters cyclists or joggers or a person who wants to stroke the fearful dog. Other dogs are afraid of stairs, being left alone or loud noises. Anxious dogs also try to escape situations and show their fear by curling their tail or putting their ears back. However, some dogs also suffer silently, as they can no longer find another way out of their fear.

Do you also have a dog that makes your everyday life difficult? Do you often feel frustrated and don't know how to support and help your dog? Do you suffer every time your dog reacts anxiously and would you like to actively work on giving you and your dog a more relaxed life? Then you are holding a book in your hand that will help you to understand your dog, his fears and his behavior in order to find the right way to deal with your anxious dog so that you can experience a more relaxed everyday life together in the future.

You will be able to recognize the causes of fear, learn to read your dog's body language and better perceive its needs, making it easier for you to communicate with your dog. In particular, however, you will learn what to look out for and what you should avoid when dealing with your traumatized dog so that you can gradually restore your dog's courage and confidence.

Traumatized dogs need time - often more than we can give them - but with a lot of patience, love, support and understanding you can offer your dog a life as free of fear as possible.

Understanding fear

WHY DOES YOUR DOG FEEL FEAR?

To understand your dog's fear, let's first look at the original function of fear as an emotion. Dogs, just like us humans, feel fear in their lives, which is normal to a certain extent. From a biological and evolutionary point of view, fear is vital for survival in dangerous situations. When danger threatens life or death, a series of emotions are activated in the brain to ensure that the body is ready for anything in order to survive. For example, the heart beats faster to distribute more blood throughout the body so that the muscles can work at peak performance if you have to flee from a life-threatening danger.

These processes are remnants of evolution - they can not only be observed in humans, but dogs have also inherited this fight for survival from wolves. Those who were able to flee faster survived - those who approached new situations with fear and caution survived if the unknown situation turned out to be dangerous. Can you now see why it sounds logical at first to be afraid of certain situations in nature? If we look at the behavior of wolves in a dangerous situation, we can observe two survival strategies, among others: flight and fight. The latter is usually the second choice. Escape is the first solution most often observed in wolves. If the wolf is restricted in its space, for example, it chooses to fight or defend itself. You can still observe these behaviors in dogs today.

The term anxiety is often confused with fear. "In the technical language of psychology and philosophy, a distinction is made between anxiety as unfounded, non-object-related and fear as object-related. In general language, however, both terms are usually used synonymously [...]"[1] . In technical terms, fear of other dogs should be referred to as fear. As soon as the danger, the other dog, is gone, the dog's body changes from a state of fear back to a normal state. Fear therefore refers to the fear of a specific object in a situation. If there is no real danger, but the dog is still in a permanent state of stress and anxiety, this is referred to as fear. In this book you will often read the colloquial term anxiety, although in most cases it is fear.

---

[1] https://www.duden.de/rechtschreibung/Angst

WHAT HAPPENS IN THE BODY WHEN THE DOG IS AFRAID?

As already mentioned, the emotion of fear is intended to prepare the body for danger. Stress hormones such as adrenaline or noradrenaline are released. The stress system is at peak performance so that the body can react as quickly as possible by fleeing or fighting. As noradrenaline is a learning amplifier, it is not without reason that anxiety behavior is referred to as a vicious circle. If your dog jumps into the lead and barks at another dog, it has been successful and repeats its strategy - our dogs are known to be opportunists. They do what is most rewarding for them.

LEARNED HELPLESSNESS

When dealing with the topic of fear, one of the terms used is "learned helplessness". If a dog is exposed to a fear trigger over a long period of time without any possibility of escaping it, the dog has no choice but to give up. "Learned helplessness refers to the phenomenon that people and animals, after experiencing helplessness or powerlessness, narrow their behavioral repertoire to such an extent that they no longer turn off these conditions that they experience as unpleasant, even though they could objectively do so."[2]

If a dog shows its fear of being left alone by howling, barking, destroying or urinating, for example, these are strategies developed by the dog to escape the situation and reduce stress. If a dog howls while being left alone, it is using this method to try to call back its social partner. If the dog is left alone for hours at a time over a longer period of time and none of these strategies help the dog out of its situation, the dog gives up and experiences helplessness. Due to negative experiences, it has developed the conviction that it can no longer change its situation with its own abilities. This is known as learned helplessness.

[2] https://lexikon.stangl.eu/1293/erlernte-hilflosigkeit/comment-page-1?fdx_switcher=desktop

TRAUMA

Fearful dogs are often traumatized. A distinction is made here between psychological and medical trauma. In medicine, a trauma is an injury to an organism caused by an external force. In psychological trauma, an organism has been traumatized by a terrible event in which it was exposed to helplessness under extreme psychological stress.

CAUSES OF FEAR

Traumatization
The reasons why a dog is anxious and traumatized are extremely complex and varied. A dog can be traumatized by bad experiences. As described above, this is an event that makes a serious incision in the dog's life. If a puppy was attacked by a large dog in its early weeks, this can be traumatizing, causing the puppy to develop a fear of other dogs in the future. A dog that has been hit by a car can develop a panic fear of traffic as a result of this trauma. However, there are also other aspects that may be responsible for your dog being fearful.

Socialization

Dogs from animal shelters in particular have experienced a lack of socialization. In order for a dog to be well socialized, it should be positively accustomed to its environment and its stimuli in its first weeks and months so that it can lead a relaxed life with its owner. This includes, for example, other people, children, the city center, visits to the vet, traffic, everyday noises, other animals and dogs. The main focus here is on calmness and composure. If a puppy spends the first few weeks of its life in isolation and does not get to know people or other stimuli, it may suffer from severe anxiety problems as an adult dog.

The term deprivation syndrome is often used in this context. Due to a lack of socialization, there is a deficit in the brain structure. The dog was isolated from the environment as a puppy and now suffers from deprivation-induced anxiety, which manifests itself in extreme stress as soon as it encounters environmental stimuli. This anxiety manifests itself in many dogs through aggressive behavior to keep the trigger away.

Mistreatment

Another cause of your dog's anxiety disorder can be mistreatment. It is understandable that dogs that have been beaten or kicked by humans are afraid of us. Abused dogs often panic when the human picks up an object, such as a belt or a key. Other dogs are so traumatized that the mere presence of a human is enough to make the dog flee.

Learned fear

In addition to these reasons for your dog's fear development, learned or associated fears can also cause your dog to be afraid of something. A classic example of an associated fear is the muzzle. If a dog is afraid of the vet, perhaps even reacts aggressively during a visit to the vet, it must always wear a muzzle during examinations. However, as it never wears a muzzle otherwise, the dog associates the muzzle with its fear of the vet and goes into a state of fear as soon as it sees a muzzle. He knows that a visit to the vet is imminent. However, learned fear can be easily overcome through counter-conditioning.

Genetics

A dog can also be genetically predisposed to react anxiously. According to a Finnish study, breed is a major contributor to anxiety. Although there are different factors that play into your dog's anxiety, genetics may be a bigger contributor than you might think. For example, 10.6% of Miniature Schnauzers were aggressive towards strangers, while only 0.4% of Labrador Retrievers were fearful. Breed-specific patterns also emerged in behavior. Border Collies showed compulsive staring and fly-snapping, whereas Miniature Schnauzers were more likely to have social anxiety, which was manifested by aggression rather than stereotypical behavior.

Although it is not possible to tell whether adult dogs are partly genetically anxious, this can be determined by testing the puppy's temperament. If you drop a bunch of keys, for example, a normal puppy will be startled briefly but will quickly recover. A puppy that is genetically anxious will take a very long time to recover, even fleeing or hiding.

Illness and pain

Before you start therapy for your anxious dog, you should definitely visit the vet first, who will examine your pet thoroughly. This will ensure that your dog's anxiety is not caused by pain or illness. Your dog's health often influences his behavior. Nutrition plays a very important role here. Serotonin deficiency or vitamin deficiency symptoms often occur when food is inadequate or insufficient. These have an effect on your dog's well-being and can be factors that contribute to your dog's anxiety. Other illnesses also have an influence on your dog's behavior. Hormonal disorders such as hypothyroidism cause your dog to become stressed and irritable very quickly. Physical illnesses such as tumors or joint problems can also cause your dog's anxiety. It is therefore advisable to have a thorough check-up with your vet before starting anxiety therapy.

Recognize fear

In order to recognize when your dog is feeling uncomfortable or anxious, you need to learn, read and interpret his body language correctly. "Learning your dog's body language is a demonstration of love that opens the door to better understanding and easier communication."[3] Before a dog escalates, he already shows his fear in many preliminary stages of his body language. Dogs communicate continuously through their bodies,

---

[3] Wilde, Nicole: Der ängstliche Hund, Stress, Unsicherheiten und Angst wirkungsvoll begegnen, Nerdlen: KYNOS VERLAG, 2008, P. 36.

usually the smallest signs are enough to know how your dog is feeling. We humans often fail to see these subtle details of our dogs' language. In the following chapter, you will learn when your dog is feeling anxious and how this is expressed through his body language.

HOW DOES ANXIETY MANIFEST ITSELF IN YOUR DOG?

Dogs often notice a fear trigger much earlier than humans. This is due to their keen sense of hearing and smell, but also to our lack of awareness of our environment. Imagine you are walking your dog in a very quiet, low-stimulus area and out of nowhere your dog is hanging on the lead and barking. You look around and ask yourself why your dog is behaving like this. After a few seconds, you notice a plastic bag blowing on the sidewalk ten meters away. Your dog seems to have noticed this immediately, whereas you only noticed it when y-our dog had already escalated. However, your dog's body language showed his fear of the bag much earlier. This is why it is particularly im-portant to know your dog's body language so that you can intervene early and break the chain of behavior until it escalates. In the following section, we differentiate between the signs and body language of a fearful dog.

Signs
Signs can be verbal and non-verbal. Audible signs of anxiety include yowling, barking, growling, whining or crying. Yawning, increased or decreased saliva production, trembling, pacing back and forth, dilated pupils and fast or slow blinking can also signal your dog's anxiety. In addition, sweaty paws, fur loss, shallow breathing, slow movements, panting, shaking, shedding, restlessness and hyperactivity are clues to recognize that your dog is uncomfortable or afraid of something. Some fearful dogs actively seek out their owner and lean against them. On the other hand, there are dogs that observe their surroundings very attentively, search for fear triggers and are no longer responsive.

Stereotypic behaviour can also be observed in some anxious or traumatized dogs. Stereotypy is a stress-induced behavior that is constantly repeated. "Dogs that are constantly anxious may develop repetitive behaviors such as licking their paws or chewing on other parts of their body." [4] If your dog exhibits similar behavior, he may be suffering from stereotypy or even obsessive-compulsive disorder. Observe your dog when he encounters a fear trigger. In most cases, one or more of these signs can be seen at a great distance from the trigger. If you can already recognize them, there is a good chance that you can support your dog in the situation at an early stage and counteract an escalation.

Body language

As soon as the first signs become noticeable in a dog, its body language and posture will quickly change. You can easily recognize an anxious dog by its tucked tail and flattened ears. You can also gauge your dog's level of anxiety here. If he only has one ear folded back or his tail is only half lowered, your dog is usually still responsive and has not yet classified the fear stimulus as a danger or threat. If, on the other hand, your dog feels

---

[4] S.36

threatened and is extremely frightened, he will pull his tail in completely and have both ears very close together.

Find out what your dog's body language looks like when he is relaxed. This will make it easier for you to recognize how his posture changes when he is afraid. The movement of the tail also reveals how your dog is feeling. A wagging tail does not always mean that your dog is happy and comfortable. In particular, if the tail wags more deeply, this may indicate that your dog is insecure and does not know what to do. Anxious dogs can also be identified by their elongated, small eyes and raised eyebrows. The pupils are dilated and you can sometimes see the whites of the eyes. The mouth closes as soon as a dog senses fear. Some dogs also raise their lips or pull the corners of their mouth back. Although ruffled neck hairs are often an indication of aggression, this can also be a sign of fear.

Many dog owners initially think their dog is aggressive, although some behavior patterns and signs of aggression are based on fear. The body posture of a fearful dog is weighted backwards, it crouches down and becomes smaller. An aggressive dog, on the other hand, puts its body weight forward, raises its ears and tail and fixates on the stimulus. You should keep in mind that in many cases aggression is based on fear, because the frightened dog has unfortunately learned that attack and defense is the best method.

HOW DOES FEAR INFLUENCE Y-OUR DOG'S BEHAVIOR?

As you learned at the beginning, wolves react to a fear stimulus with the fight-or-flight response. These conflict solutions, also known as the "4 Fs", can be divided into four categories in dogs today: The first two strategies represent attack, or fight, and the second option is flight. The third category is freeze/faint, while the last conflict strategy is fiddle. Dog owners often perceive the latter as fooling around, although the function of this behavior is to reduce a dangerous situation for the dog. In this context, sniffing, jumping or wiggling are de-escalating actions to make it clear to the other dog that it is not a threat in the hope that the situation will resolve. Appeasement signals are therefore intended to communicate to the other person that you are not a threat. Dogs also use these signals to express that they feel uncomfortable.

Yawning is often misunderstood here. Although it is a sign of tiredness, it is also an expression of stress, anxiety or submission. Many dogs do not always scratch and sniff because they suddenly have an itch or because they smell something good. These signals can also serve to appease and mean that your dog needs a break or is feeling uncomfortable. Licking its own lips is also an indication of discomfort. The dog licks its own muzzle with its tongue. You can often observe this behavior when someone pets your dog and it is too much for him.

A very conspicuous appeasement signal is turning away or looking away. Direct staring or fixation signals danger among dogs. It is therefore understandable that a fearful dog will often turn away from threatening stimuli to show that it is not in danger. Pay attention to the situations in which your dog shows the signals just listed. This will help you to find out what frightens your dog. Accordingly, you can avoid situations at an early stage that cause your dog so much stress and fear that he has to use the defense, the fight, of the four

Fs as a solution strategy. On the other hand, reward preliminary stages such as appeasement signals. These help your dog to lower his stress level
and choose other solutions than attacking.

Your dog never stops communicating - he just
does it in a different language. If you get to know
them, you can support your dog, understand his
needs and work on the cause of his fear. Your dog
will start to trust you because he knows that you
understand him and his feelings and make good
decisions for him.

IDENTIFYING THE ANXIETY TRIG-
GERS

As soon as you know your dog's body language,
you will be able to filter out the fear triggers very
well. However, this alone is not enough to know
exactly what your dog is afraid of. For example, if
he is afraid of other people, this is initially a very
general statement and requires even more sensitivity. Many factors play a role in fear stimuli. For
example, a dog may only be afraid of men, but not
of women. An item of clothing such as a black hat,
an umbrella, a bucket, sunglasses or a walking

stick may also be the trigger. Below you will learn about some triggers so that you can get an idea of which stimuli can be frightening for your dog. It is helpful to create a table in which you list possible triggers. You can also add how your dog reacts to them in terms of body language and what helps him to get through the situation.

According to the Finnish study "Prevalence, comorbidity and breed differences in fear dogs in 13,700 Finnish pet dogs", 32% of dogs suffer from noise sensitivity, making fear of noise the most common among dogs. As there are countless noises in our environment, only the most common triggers are mentioned here. These include thunderstorms, cars/trucks/trailers, fireworks, knocking, ringing, unexpected noises such as something falling, keys, beeps, sirens, rolling garbage cans, shopping carts, closing car doors and the sound of people arguing, screaming, laughing or shouting.

Dogs can also react anxiously to certain movements. These can be both fast and slow. Your dog may therefore be afraid of a slow-moving hand, sudden movements such as a person standing up or a door swinging open. Many dogs are also afraid of fast stimulus movements such as skateboarders or cyclists. Strange gaits of other people, such as shuffling or stamping, also unsettle some dogs. Light and shadow are also movements that can trigger fear.

According to the Finnish study, around 17% of domestic dogs are afraid of other dogs. Your dog can be afraid of any dog, but many fearful dogs differentiate between other dogs that pose a danger to them. Gender, size, color and breed characteristics often play a role in the classification. Some dogs are also afraid of conspecifics of a certain color or with special ears, such as drooping, standing or cropped ears. Dogs with a docked tail are often unable to assess conspecifics and are unsettled because this dog cannot send signals and communicate via its tail. It can also be important whether the other dog is neutered or not.

One of the biggest factors in dog encounters is the leash as a fear trigger. Some dogs feel restricted in their body language and space and develop leash aggression towards other dogs. Similarly, dogs running loose can instill fear in your dog, whereas dogs on a lead are no particular threat to him. During the interaction, your dog may also feel harassed and show signs of fear. Sniffing the rear end, staring, approaching from behind or a fellow dog running towards your dog head-on are perceived by fearful dogs as unpleasant or as a danger.

Just as fearful dogs can differentiate the threat level of their fellow dogs, this is often also the case with humans. Gender, age, skin color and build can all be fear triggers for your dog. Perhaps your dog was mistreated by a person with a large build, which is why he is only afraid of these people. Often dogs have had bad experiences with children or have even been traumatized, which is why age can also be of great importance. In addition, various dogs show fearful reactions towards certain people such as the letter carrier, the delivery man, the vet or the gardener. Strangers generally cause stress and anxiety for traumatized dogs. You are unable to assess your dog and do not pay attention to its body language. Leaning over the dog, approaching it directly, staring at it and holding out your hand all have a threatening effect on dogs.

If a dog has been kicked a lot before, it may panic at the slightest movement of your foot.

Fearful or traumatized dogs are reluctant to be touched, especially if the touch comes from above or as a surprise. Your dog may also be afraid of touching certain parts of the body or being picked up or held. For example, some dogs are afraid of having their claws touched, as they may associate this with having their claws clipped. Similarly, brushing can cause your dog anxiety. There are an infinite number of stimuli and situations that can frighten your dog. It is important to determine the exact trigger so that you can work specifically on the cause of the anxiety. To do this, you need to consider all environmental factors during a fear reaction. The smallest details can shed light on why your dog is behaving in this way. For training and therapy to be successful, the trigger must be correctly identified. Once you have observed and studied your dog in detail, you can start training and find the right way to deal with your fearful dog.

Dealing with fear the right way

Now you have learned how to read your dog's body language and behavior and how to identify his fear triggers. In the following, you will learn how to deal with your fearful dog correctly and how to treat his fear. Keep in mind, however, that every dog is individual and depending on your dog's level of anxiety, you should consult a professional dog trainer.

HOW DOES MY DOG LEARN?

In order to understand and comprehend what you should avoid and encourage when dealing with your dog, you first need to know how your dog learns. As you already know, our dogs are constantly associating and linking signals and situations. Dogs are always learning - so it is particularly important that you know how this happens in order to work on his fear. At some point, your dog has learned that a certain stimulus or signal is a threat to him. So that you can link this stimulus in a new and positive way, you should know in advance how dogs make associations.

Classical conditioning
The learning of a stimulus in learning psychology is "classical conditioning". A stimulus that was previously neutral now takes on a meaning for your dog. This meaning can be positive or negative and thus trigger different emotions. Conditioning is therefore a stimulus-response pattern. All signals that you teach your dog have been conditioned. Your doorbell is also a wonderful example of classical conditioning - your dog has learned that

it announces a visitor, which may mean stress. He therefore associates the doorbell with negative feelings. After all, a dog doesn't bark when the doorbell rings for no reason.

Operant conditioning

In addition to classical conditioning, there is also operant conditioning: learning through trial and error. A dog shows a behavior whose consequences determine whether it repeats the behavior or not. A behavior that has good consequences will be shown more often in the future. If unpleasant consequences follow a behavior, the dog will perform it less often. Operant conditioning can also be divided into four quadrants:

1. *Positive reinforcement* means that something *pleasant* is *added.* A behavior that is positively reinforced is shown more often. This triggers the emotion of pleasure in your dog. For example, if I reward calmly looking at a fear trigger, I reinforce this behavior and the dog will show it more often or for longer in the future. It is important that your dog also perceives the reward as a reinforcer. For example, some dogs prefer a toy to food. Other

dogs, on the other hand, find sniffing a reward desirable.

2. The *positive punishment* describes the *addition of* something *unpleasant.* An avoidance behavior is then established. The dog shows the behavior that is being punished less. This triggers the emotion of fear or anxiety. Imagine spraying your dog with water every time he barks at other dogs. Your dog will reduce this behavior in the future and bark less because he is afraid of the consequence of "getting wet". In the next chapter, you will find out why this part of operant conditioning is problematic and why you should definitely refrain from using it with your dog.

3. *Negative reinforcement* means that something *unpleasant* is *removed. This creates* the emotion of relief and the behavior is performed more frequently. If you teach your dog the sit signal by pressing on the dog's bottom until it sits down, your dog learns that the "sit" behavior is worthwhile because the unpleasantness, in this case the pressure on the bottom, stops with the desired behavior, the "sit". Negative reinforcement occurs with your anxious dog, for example, when he barks at another dog on the lead out of fear and

is successful. He learns that the unpleasant stimulus "dog" disappears as a result of the "bark" behavior. Your dog is then relieved and will show this behavior more often in the future.

4. *Negative punishment represents* the last quadrant of operant conditioning. Here, in contrast to negative reinforcement, something *pleasant* is *removed*, whereupon the behavior is shown less. Your dog feels frustrated. An example of negative punishment is jumping up at people if you then ignore your dog or turn away. By not paying attention to your dog and thus removing the pleasant consequence, he will show the behavior of jumping up on other people less because it is not rewarding.

YOU SHOULD AVOID

One of the most important aspects that you should avoid when handling and training your dog is triggering a state of fear. If possible, you should work below your dog's reaction threshold. As soon as your dog reacts anxiously, he is no longer in the thinking part of his brain. He is simply too stressed and frightened to be able to learn sustainably.

In addition, his fear and behavior will be reinforced every time he is helplessly exposed to a fear trigger. Pay attention to the distance at which your dog still behaves reasonably calmly towards the trigger and train your dog at this distance. This is the basic prerequisite for training and anxiety therapy. In this chapter, you will find out what else you should avoid when dealing with your anxious dog.

Punishment and violence
If you have a fearful or traumatized dog, you should definitely avoid punishment when handling your dog. Many dogs are frightened for this very reason. They have experienced terrible things and have been traumatized. There are also many factors that speak against the use of punishment. Let's stick with the example of your dog being afraid of other dogs. As soon as he sees a dog, he jumps into the lead and barks. You could now punish this behavior with a water bottle, various startle stimuli, a tug on the lead or by physically blocking it. At first, your dog will most likely stop barking. But has the punishment improved his emotional state? With punishment, you are

merely inhibiting the symptoms of a cause that lies much deeper. You have only scratched the surface of what we see and find unpleasant. You may have solved your own problem - but not your dog's problem. Your dog is still fruitfully afraid of other dogs and now also of his own owner, as he has made the situation worse for him.

It could also be that your dog finds other dogs even more threatening in the future than he already does, as he associates the appearance of other dogs with your punishment, which triggers negative emotions in your dog. This is precisely the danger of punishment: it is almost impossible to carry it out precisely so that your dog associates the punishment correctly. In addition, you have previously learned that an unwanted behavior is reinforced through repetition and success. In order to punish your dog for the unwanted behavior, he must first perform it, which establishes the behavior each time.

Unwanted behavior is also often referred to as "misbehavior". However, in our view, this is just wrong behavior, which is usually the best solution for the dog to master the situation. Your dog would never question the misbehavior itself, because in its eyes it is behaving completely correctly. Dogs do not differentiate between right and wrong: they do what is worthwhile for them. If your dog barks at another dog out of fear and the other dog then disappears, then the "misbehavior" was worthwhile for your dog. He doesn't see it as wrong, it's a strategy to resolve the situation. Do you remember the wolf's flight-or-fight response? Then you can understand very well why your dog shows unwanted behavior towards fear triggers. After all, he has no choice but to flee. If this is not possible because your dog is on a lead, for example, his second solution is to attack forwards. Once you have understood this topic, it becomes clear that punishment only remedies the symptoms of the cause, but not the actual problem.

If you want to help your dog overcome his fears and redirect his emotions towards triggers, you should know that this may take a long time. You need to build trust, know your dog's needs and body language so that your dog knows he can rely on you and your decisions. You can't achieve all these things with punishment. It has been scientifically proven that positive reinforcement and avoiding punishment is the most effective way of dealing with your dog in the long term.

Flooding

Have you ever heard well-intentioned advice such as "He has to learn that!" or "He has to get through that!" regarding your dog's fear? If you're out and about with your anxious dog, you've probably heard these or similar tips from other people. However, you should be particularly careful with advice of this kind. This line of thought implies a type of anxiety therapy that you should stay away from. Flooding means that the dog is exposed to a fear trigger until it gives up from exhaustion and no longer seems to be afraid of the trigger. The aim of this therapy is for the dog to realize after flooding that the fear trigger is not as bad as it seems. This form of therapy is controversial even in humans and should especially not be used on animals. Flooding may only be used as anxiety therapy with the explicit consent of the person concerned. You should not try flooding on your dog, as the consequences can be devastating: Trust in the owner is destroyed, learned helplessness develops, your dog feels mortal fear and his anxiety disorder worsens, not to mention the health damage that can result from all the stress.

Imagine that your dog is terrified of traffic. You could now sit down on the road with your dog, who is screaming out of sheer fear, and wait until he is completely exhausted and no longer shows any behavior. However, your dog will suffer extreme psychological damage from this experience. All strategies to escape the situation will not work. When he then seeks help from his social partner, he is not met with the support and understanding he had hoped for, but with ignorance. Can you see how helpless, lost and frightened your dog must feel when flooding? The next time your dog encounters traffic, it is highly likely that he will associate this trauma with the trigger and his fear of traffic will be even greater and the wound even deeper. Are you afraid of spiders? Imagine if your closest social partner put you in a room full of spiders without your consent and only got you out when you were completely exhausted and helpless on the floor. Your trust would be broken and your fear of spiders would probably not be cured after this traumatic experience. Treat your dog as you would like to be treated and always ask yourself the question: "Would I like to be my own dog?"

Belief in dominance

Alongside various other pieces of advice, you've probably heard phrases like "You have to show y-our dog who's boss!" or "You have to clarify the hierarchy first!". In the dog world, the belief in the dominance theory still persists - even though it has already been refuted by its own inventor. Particularly in the case of difficult dogs, it is often said that they are not subordinate to their human, the "pack leader", and that harmonious coexistence is therefore not possible. The dog always tries to become the "alpha dog" or "leader" and to dominate its human in order to take the highest position in the hierarchy. Dog owners are advised to use violent techniques and methods to assert their authority and subordinate the dog through intimidation. Regardless of whether you have a fearful dog or not, you should definitely keep your distance from this topic. These ideas damage your relationship with your dog and are simply wrong views that can be scientifically refuted. Dog trainers who engage in these practices use the construct of "dominance" as a justification for using violent training techniques. In the following, you will learn why the dominance theory is not a matter of fact, but of opinion, and why you should refrain from using these methods with your dog.

The term dominance was originally coined in the 1920s. The Norwegian researcher Schjelderup-Ebbe observed the relationships and social behavior between chickens. The competition for food is said to take place in a certain system: The highest ranking chicken in the hierarchy pecked away all other chickens, the next highest chicken pecked away all others except the highest, and so on. Over time, this hierarchy was also transferred to other creatures, such as the hierarchy in wolves and ultimately dogs. The dominance theory in wolves is based on observations of unrelated wolves in captivity. Here you can already see the problem with this study: Wolves in captivity are restricted and behave differently than in the wild. According to the latest findings, wolves in the wild do not live in a strictly hierarchical pack. They live in a social structure that is similar to a family group. This means that wolves in a pack do not constantly compete with each other for the highest ranking and try to become the "alpha wolf".

It is true that dominance is linked to resources and is therefore not a trait. An animal can behave dominantly towards conspecific A. If it now encounters conspecific B, the animal may not behave dominantly towards conspecific B, even though it would claim the resource for itself when interacting with conspecific A and would therefore behave dominantly. Dominance is therefore not a character trait, but a behavior. This behavior can only take place within a species. Our dogs cannot therefore dominate us, as we are humans and do not belong to the "dog" species. We do not form a pack with our dogs - we are part of a social group. The dominance theory can therefore be scientifically refuted.

Nevertheless, many dog trainers today still justify their methods with the belief in dominance and go through so-called "rank reduction programs" to consolidate their position as pack leader. The dog is therefore only allowed to eat after the pack leader, because the "alpha" is always the first to have access to resources. He must always make way when you walk through the room as the pack leader. You must be the first through the door, your dog should always come second. Your dog must never end the game himself.

If the dog tries to be "dominant", the owner reacts by pinching the lips, biting the ear or, in the worst case, with the alpha throw. In the alpha throw, the dog is jerkily turned onto its back, which is supposed to be a way of demonstrating power between wolves. However, the difference here is that a wolf voluntarily submits to the dominant wolf and is not forced into this position. Your dog will never associate the alpha litter with its ancestors - it merely learns that its own owner, who should be a trusted person, causes it mortal fear.

Behavioral problems that are based on fear can only be changed by changing the feelings towards the trigger. Outdated and disproved myths such as the belief in dominance do not help your dog or you to experience a relaxed everyday life. You should therefore reject the belief in dominance under all circumstances and avoid such training methods when dealing with your traumatized dog.

Ten things you should avoid when dealing with your anxious dog

1. you should never force your dog into a situation in which he becomes afraid. Forcing your dog to do something he is terrified of can destroy your relationship and trust forever. Interaction and training with your dog should be voluntary.

2. avoid pulling and tugging on the lead. This can trigger negative emotions in your dog.

3. do not go for long walks, especially in areas where there is a lot of stimulation. Go for walks where there is not much going on. Avoid crowded cities or crowded places.

4. you should not let your dog run free immediately or only lead it on a collar. There is a risk that your dog will be frightened by a stimulus and flee. He could also slip out of the collar and run away. A frightened dog is full of adrenaline and is under such a high level of stress that it loses its orientation and cannot find its way back home or even runs onto a road in its madness. Secure your dog with a safety harness and use a drag line for running free.

5 Avoid as much stress as possible and build up distance from triggers.

6. you should definitely give your dog space and not pressurize or physically restrict him.

7. do not take your dog's food away, leave him alone during this time. Otherwise you could provoke a resource defense.

8. avoid a large number of visitors. Fearful dogs are usually afraid of strangers or unknown people and do not know how to deal with them. Tell your visitors not to disturb your dog. Stand up for your dog, no matter what reactions or advice you hear in response. Your dog will realize that you have the situation under control and are speaking for him.

9 Do not ignore your dog when he is afraid. This can lead to a loss of the trust you have built up and permanently damage your relationship.

10. do not punish your dog when he shows unwanted behavior. Behind every undesirable behavior is an emotion that directs the behavior. Refrain from using force or impatience when dealing with your dog. Instead, praise good behavior and work your way to success in small steps.

WHAT YOU SHOULD PROMOTE

Now that you have learned what you should avoid when dealing with your dog, you can start encouraging and training your dog. You will learn how you can make your everyday life with your anxious dog easier, what the basic requirements for good anxiety therapy are and how you can treat your dog correctly and support him in his anxiety so that he can go through life with more courage in the future. Bear in mind, however, that it can take a long time for your dog's anxiety to improve - after all, good anxiety therapy also needs to last a long time. A person cannot simply get over and forget a trauma within six weeks. Your dog may never become a "normal" dog, but if you understand and encourage the following points when dealing with your dog, the chances are good that your dog will be able to overcome many of its fears together with you.

Management, trust and patience

To improve your everyday life, you must first and foremost practice management. If possible, you should reduce general everyday stress and avoid situations that make your dog anxious. You should expose your dog to stimuli to which your dog reacts anxiously as rarely as possible. Why? Because unwanted behavior is reinforced with every repetition. You also need to build trust with your dog. Would you trust a person who deliberately forces you into a situation that you are absolutely terrified of and panic about? Show your dog that you can read his body language and that he can count on your support. Even though it is often difficult to avoid triggers, in most cases there is always a way to avoid the stimulus if you notice it early.

If another dog comes towards you, you could move into a field or the woods. If this is not possible, you can also simply turn around and walk back until you are able to keep your distance. Signals such as the reorientation signal or the change of direction signal can help you to manage the situation in such moments.

The reorientation signal is set up in a similar way to a clicker. You give the signal, whereupon something very exciting and great happens for your dog. This could be playing a game together, chasing after a treat or liverwurst from a tube. Your dog doesn't have to do anything. The signal should draw your dog's attention to you in dangerous situations so that you can then turn around and walk away from the fear trigger, for example. If a stranger approaches your dog, which frightens your dog, you can give the reorientation signal, for example. For the change of direction signal, stand in front of the dog sitting in your direction. Now walk past him. If he turns around and comes with you, reward him. Later you can add the signal word, for example "turn" or "turn around". This teaches your dog to change direction when given a signal. These two signals can be a great support in everyday life if they have been built up well and in detail. You can avoid many situations with this management.

It is important that you always keep your ears and eyes open. Nevertheless, it can always happen that your dog reacts with fear. If the reaction is mild, you can try to distract your dog with tasty treats and get him out of the situation. If your dog has an extreme reaction, you should communicate calmness. It will not help your dog if you become hysterical in the situation. Leave the area as quickly as possible and return home. After an anxiety reaction, your dog's body needs a very long time to reduce the stress hormones. Your dog is still on alert and continuing the walk could risk another, even more severe relapse.

When it comes to training your anxious dog, you also have to work on yourself for the most part. It's human nature to focus on the negative and get frustrated when something doesn't work right away. Unfortunately, patience is the be-all and end-all when dealing with your anxious dog. Remember what your dog may have had to go through. Your dog is not displaying the unwanted behavior just to annoy you. There is always a reason why your dog is behaving the way he is. It is up to you to remain calm and patient and identify the cause of the unwanted behavior.

If your dog has had a fearful reaction, think about your own actions first, change your training plan or take a few steps back in training. Sometimes we humans are very overzealous and take too many steps at once because of a success. Your dog will quickly feel overwhelmed. Help your dog instead of being angry with him. If you are patient and calm with your dog, you will achieve success more quickly. Don't set your goals too high - then you won't have high expectations. The small successes are usually the biggest steps towards your goal.

Rest and relaxation

"The ability to relax is one of the most useful skills a nervous dog can learn." [5] Anxious dogs need a lot of time to process what they have experienced. They are often exposed to extreme stress outside. Imagine feeling stress, anxiety and panic every time you go out the door. This robs you of energy and concentration, so your body needs sleep to recharge its batteries and process everything properly. It is therefore very important that you find a balance between training, everyday life and rest

---

[5] Wilde, Nicole: Der ängstliche Hund, Stress, Unsicherheiten und Angst wirkungsvoll begegnen, Nerdlen: KYNOS VERLAG, 2008, P.119

for your dog. You should make sure that your dog can sleep during the day. Adult dogs need around 15 to 20 hours of sleep and relaxation a day.

We are increasingly hearing that anxious and traumatized dogs find it very difficult to calm down. Ritualized routines and certainty of expectations can help your dog to calm down better. You can also actively work on calmness and relaxation with some exercises. Your dog should have a place to retreat to, such as a dog crate or basket. Reward your dog when he lies down there and reinforce calm, relaxed behavior. However, you should not reward him exuberantly: A gentle "very good" or a treat is perfectly adequate.

Conditioned relaxation is another way to relax your dog in everyday life. You already know what classical conditioning is. Your dog learns every second of its life and constantly links other stimuli with feelings or actions. You can also link a signal with relaxation. If your dog feels relaxed by a massage, stroking or brushing, you can say the signal word beforehand, for example "Easy", and then perform the relaxing action. It is important that your dog is really in a relaxed state. Repeat this exercise several times. Soon the signal alone will trigger relaxed emotions in your dog. If your dog does not want to be touched or does not feel comfortable when you stroke or massage him, you can simply repeat the word while your dog is lying relaxed in his basket anyway.

There are also visual signals that your dog associates with relaxation. This can be a cloth, a blanket or acoustic signals such as the radio or classical music. Olfactory stimuli, for example lavender oil, can also be associated with calmness by your dog. Simply place a scarf with the scent next to your relaxed dog. He will soon associate the smell with being relaxed, which can be helpful if your dog has separation anxiety, for example. You can use the "Easy" relaxation signal in situations where your dog's excitement level is so high that he is no longer responsive. The signal is not a cure, whereupon your dog will lie down and sleep, but it can trigger positive emotions in your dog that bring him down a few levels on the arousal scale so that he is responsive again and you can ask for an alternative behavior or leave the situation. You should always recharge the relaxation signal so that your dog does not start to associate the signal with the fear trigger.

Social Support

Your dog may also actively seek social support from you. Unfortunately, the myth still persists that if you give your dog attention and support in his fear, you will increase his anxiety. Many dog owners even recommend ignoring the dog completely and pretending that nothing bad is happening while the dog lies on the floor like a heap of misery.

Why is this attitude problematic? Social support means that caregivers provide assistance in frightening situations. This highly social behavior can be observed not only in humans, but also in other animal species. If your dog seeks protection from you and is then ignored by its attachment figure, this can seriously damage your relationship. In the worst case scenario, it can even lead to a loss of trust. Meanwhile, it has been disproven that social contact such as attention, physical contact or treats increases your dog's fear. A positive emotion cannot reinforce a negative emotion. In addition, physical contact leads to a release of oxytocin, which reduces the stress hormone cortisol.

Social support does not mean that you should now grab and stroke your dog when he is afraid. Many dogs also don't like being touched during a fear-inducing situation. This could cause more stress and give your dog negative feelings. If it helps your dog and he may even press close to y-our body and seek protection, you should also give him the security. It is also important that you remain calm yourself when your dog encounters a fear trigger. If you panic yourself, this mood can be transferred to your dog.

Desensitization
Desensitization is an anxiety therapy in which you expose your dog to a trigger at a great distance. Your dog should not show any fear reaction. In this way, you get your dog used to the presence of the fear trigger at a long distance. If you work in small steps, your dog will get used to the trigger over time and you can slowly reduce the distance. Desensitization helps your dog to overcome his fears in a nice way. Desensitization is therefore the opposite of flooding - which you should avoid at all costs.

If you know your dog's body language, you will quickly realize at what distance your dog feels comfortable and when you can take a step forward. During desensitization, you should pay attention to certain factors. First of all, as already mentioned, you should estimate the distance at which your dog will react reasonably calmly to the trigger. Another factor is the angle at which you approach the trigger. Many dogs find it easier if you walk around the trigger instead of approaching it head-on. Your dog will probably perceive it as a threat if a person leans over him to pet him. Tell the person that your dog will feel more comfortable if they crouch down on the ground and let your dog come to them.

The speed of the stimulus also plays a major role. A dog that walks past you slowly is more bearable for your dog than a running dog. Your own speed also has an influence on your dog's well-being. Make your dog feel calm and walk past stimuli at a normal, slow pace. If you speed up because you are afraid that your dog will react to the trigger, your dog will notice your restlessness. Finally, the characteristic of the fear trigger is important: increase the difficulty slowly. Practice first in the presence of a trigger that does not behave dynamically. Is your dog afraid of screaming children? Then start training in the presence of quiet children.

All these factors have one thing in common: you should work in small steps and not overwhelm your dog. Show your dog understanding and patience and let him know that you understand his needs. Only in this way will your dog learn to trust you in order to rebuild his courage in anxious situations.

Desensitization is particularly useful for separation anxiety. If your dog is already in an anxious state when you just reach for your rucksack, put on your jacket or pick up your keys, you should first reduce and desensitize these signals. Put your things in your rucksack and then sit down. Reach for your keys several times a day and put on your shoes without going outside. Your dog should learn that these signals no longer have any meaning and are no reason to panic. If your dog behaves calmly as soon as you pack your bag or take your key, you can train him in small steps to go to the door, open the door and finally go outside.

Counter-conditioning

The final technique for overcoming your dog's fears explained in this book is counter-conditioning. In counter-conditioning, a stimulus-response link is re-linked through slow steps. A stimulus that previously triggered negative emotions in your dog is conditioned to positive emotions. If your dog is afraid of a broom because it may have been hit or mistreated with it before, counter-conditioning is used to change the feelings and emotions towards the fear trigger so that your dog gradually associates a positive emotion with the broom and is no longer afraid of it. For example, you could reward your dog with a treat every time he looks calmly at the broom.

The next step is to reduce the distance in small steps until your dog can sit relaxed next to the brush. It is important that you do not have a negative effect on your dog during this fear therapy and only reward your dog when it is calm in the presence of the trigger. If your dog reacts tensely or anxiously, you have taken too many steps and you need to increase the distance to the stimulus. You should never lure your dog to a fear trigger. Your dog might take the food, but then panic and, in the worst case, associate the food with the fear trigger. If you proceed in small steps, work at a distance, pay attention to your dog's needs and train below your dog's fear threshold, counter-conditioning can be successful very quickly. One example of the use of stimulus counter-conditioning is "click for gaze", which you will learn how to do in the next chapter.

Click for view

To carry out this type of counter-conditioning, you need a clicker or a marker word. The sound from the clicker or your chosen marker word, for example "Yes", "Top" or "Click", is conditioned to a reward. Your dog thus learns that the click or your marker word is a confirmation of his behavior and heralds a reward. Take about 15 to 20 treats and stand in front of your dog. Click or say your marker word and immediately give your dog a treat. Your dog doesn't have to do anything, because he should only learn that the click is a reward. You should first set up the clicker in a quiet environment, for example at home or in the garden. Once your dog has understood that the click or the marker word means something great, you can now vary the reward, increase the distractions and change the location. As soon as the click triggers happy expectations in your dog and he orients himself towards you, you have successfully set up the clicker and can now confirm desired behavior and communicate better with your dog.

You can now use the marker word especially in situations in which your dog encounters a fear trigger. Train according to the motto "Every dog always shows good behavior before it shows unwanted behavior" and mark the behavior that your dog does great. "Click for look" is a training method that you can apply to all stimuli in order to counter-condition and build up an alternative behavior. The purpose of "click for gaze" is initially to reward calmly looking at the stimulus. For example, if your dog sees another dog, you immediately catch this behavior with a secondary reinforcer, a clicker or a marker word. You reward the desired behavior, in this case calmly looking at the stimulus. If the clicker or marker word is well conditioned to a reward, your dog will then look at you and wait for its reward. However, this is where many dog owners drop out, as their dog will not take food outside.

Dogs are biologically designed to work for food. If your dog does not accept treats, there is often a reason for this. For example, it may mean that the distance to the stimulus is too short and therefore an emotion such as fear, frustration or excitement is getting in the way, inhibiting your dog's appetite. Your dog is too stressed to learn effectively. Have you ever tried to learn under fear, frustration or stress? You need to find your dog's threshold to where he is able to calmly observe the fear trigger and learn that it is worth staying calm and cooperating with you. Over time, you will realize that you can reduce the distance to the stimulus more and more.

In the second training step, the marker word is omitted. Your dog sees a fear trigger and expects the click or the marker word from you. If this does not come, your dog will automatically look at you because he will wonder where his reward for looking is. This moment, when your dog turns and looks at you, is now rewarded. Over time, your dog's fear triggers will become a situation that your dog associates positively. Fear triggers such as other dogs or people now take on a different meaning for your dog: his previously established chain of behavior, such as fixing, barking and jumping into the leash, has been broken. Now your dog associates the fear triggers with positive emotions.

In addition to "click for look", you can of course also use the marker word to confirm all other behaviors that you think are good. For example, if your dog is afraid of stairs, you can approach the stairs step by step, create positive emotions at the sight of stairs and give your dog the courage to approach the stairs. If your dog is afraid of having its ears, claws or paws examined by you, you can use clicker training to overcome this fear using the same approach. However, remember that you should not confuse clicker training with luring. Clicker training rewards voluntary behavior.

As you can see, you should not do without the marker word when training your fearful dog. It is the bridge between humans and dogs and the opportunity to communicate with our dogs in a great and joyful way.

Important words at the end: Accept your dog

Finding the right way to handle your dog often sounds easy on paper, but in reality it's usually different. After all, we are only human and we make mistakes. However, the fact that you are dealing with the theory and practice of this topic shows that you want to deal with your dog's fears and understand them. You are already on the right track. Just as our dogs learn through repetition, you as a dog owner must first practise how you deal with your dog and his fear. Regression is normal and it is understandable if you sometimes feel close to despair. Building trust and a bond takes time.

You will probably never know why your dog is so frightened and traumatized. It no longer matters, because he is safe and in good hands in your presence. In the end, that's exactly what counts. Enjoy the time you have been given with your dog. The most important thing for a better everyday life and bond with your dog is that you accept him for who he is. You can probably never turn your dog into a completely anxiety-free or normal dog. The sooner you accept your dog in all its facets, the more pleasant and harmonious your relationship will be and the calmer your everyday life will be. Focus on the successes and enjoy the wonderful experiences with your dog. If you encourage and strengthen these moments, your dog will also become braver and more self-confident and learn to trust you even in frightening situations.

Bibliography

- Author unknown: Deprivation syndrome (hospitalism) in dogs, https://auslandstierschutz.jimdo.com/infos-zu-den-tieren/angsthunde/deprivation/, status: unknown (retrieved on 21.09.2021)
- Gutmann, Monika: Clicker training, other ways to communicate with your dog, Schwarzenbek: Cadmos Verlag GmbH, 2010/2011
- Author unknown: Socialization: how does a puppy become a confident dog?, https://www.tierfreund.de/sozialisierung/, status: unknown (retrieved 21.09.2021)

• Wilde, Nicole: Der ängstliche Hund, Stress, Unsicherheiten und Angst wirkungsvoll begegnen, Nerdlen: KYNOS VERLAG, 2008

• Frank, Rolf C., Grauss, Madeleine: Hab' keine Angst mein Hund, Recognizing and reducing fears in dogs, Brunsbek: Cadmos Verlag GmbH, 2008

• Rütter, Martin: Angst bei Hunden, Umgang mit ängstlichen und traumatisierten Hunden, Stuttgart: Franckh Komsos Verlag, 2018

• Author unknown: Dog in conflict - your dog can react to threats with these four options, https://www.haustiermagazin.com/hund-im-konflikt-vier-f/, as of 08.11.2018 (retrieved on 21.09.2021)

• Greife, Leonie: Is your dog anxious? What genes have to do with it, https://www.deine-tierwelt.de/magazin/ist-dein-hund-aengstlich-was-die-gene-damit-zu-tun-haben/, as of 08.11.2020 (retrieved on 21.09.2021)

• Salonen, Milla, Sulkama, Sini, Mikkola, Salla, Puurunen, Jenni, Hakanen, Emma, Tiira, Katriina, Araujo, César, Lohi, Hannes: Prevalence, Comorbodity, and breed differences in canine anxiety in 13,799 Finnish pet dogs, https://www.nature.com/articles/s41598-020-59837-z, as of 05.03.2020 (accessed on 21.09.2021)

• Hess, Carolin: Social support: Why you should be there for your dog, when he is afraid and what to consider, https://www.easy-dogs.net/social-support/, as of 13.12.2019 (retrieved on 21.09.2021)

• Hoffmann, Carolin: The fearful animal welfare dog from abroad, https://www.trainieren-statt-dominieren.de/blog/angst-unsicherheit/der-a-engstliche-tierschutzhund-aus-dem-ausland, as of 27.11.2020 (retrieved on 21.09.2021)

• Blaschke-Berthold, Dr. Ute: Conditioned relaxation in dogs: structure, application in everyday life and sources of error in training, https://www.easy-dogs.net/konditionierte-ent-spannung/ Status: 20.11.2018 (retrieved on 21.09.2021)